I0236084

IN MEMORY OF

_____

ABOUT THE AUTHOR

Shaela Mauger and Harpermartin

Born and raised in Wagga Wagga in regional New South Wales, Shaela has pursued her love of graphic design through university and began her career as a designer for a local printer.

Since becoming a mother, Shaela has fine-tuned her design passion towards what is now most important to her: loved ones, and cherishing the time we have with them. Now, after half a decade of having her own design business, Shaela has launched Harpermartin · paying homage to her parents' family names · and this series of keepsake books, created to celebrate life and love in all its forms.

The series is available at www.harpermartin.com.au

Copyright © Shaela Mauger 2018
Original cover painting copyright © Fay Mifsud 2018

All rights reserved. No part of this publication may be reproduced, stored in a retrieval system or transmitted, in any form or by any means, electronic, mechanical, photocopying, recording or otherwise, without prior permission of the copyright holder.

ISBN 978·0·6482778·2·8

Remembering Me

—— SIBLING EDITION ——

By Shaela Mauger

Cover watercolour painting by Faenerys
www.faenerys.com

I HAVE ANOTHER SIBLING

I have another sibling that the world cannot see.
My greatest wish is that my sibling was here to play and talk with me.
I have another sibling that looks out for me everyday,
And makes sure my family and I are going along okay.
I have another sibling, beautiful as can be,
A precious part of my family no longer here with me.
I have another sibling, I am very proud to say,
That is why there are rainbows after the skies are grey.
I have another sibling I love with all my heart,
Today, tomorrow and every day we are apart.

SHAELA MAUGER
Founder, Harpermartin

TABLE OF CONTENTS

PREFACE

This sibling book was designed to honour the precious bond formed between siblings. Even though the sibling may not be with them today they are forever on their minds and in their hearts.

It gives children an avenue to express their feelings through drawing, writing and prompts.

May this beautiful book allow you to spend precious time as a family honouring your baby gone too soon.

With love,

Shaela xx

Founder, Harpermartin

ALL ABOUT YOU...

Your name: _____

The meaning/history of your name: _____

_____

Date: _____ Time: _____

Weight: _____ Length: _____

Hair colour: _____

Eye colour: _____

YOUR SIBLINGS

AFFIX PHOTO HERE

My name is:_____

I am _____ years old

My birthdate is:_____

My favourite hobbies are: _____

_____

My favourite things are: _____

_____

YOUR SIBLINGS

AFFIX PHOTO HERE

My name is:_____

I am _____ years old

My birthdate is:_____

My favourite hobbies are: _____

_____

My favourite things are: _____

_____

YOUR SIBLINGS

AFFIX PHOTO HERE

My name is:_____

I am _____ years old

My birthdate is:_____

My favourite hobbies are: _____

_____

My favourite things are: _____

_____

YOUR SIBLINGS

AFFIX PHOTO HERE

My name is: _____

I am _____ years old

My birthdate is: _____

My favourite hobbies are: _____

_____

My favourite things are: _____

_____

By: _____ Date: _____

By: _____ Date: _____

By: _____ Date: _____

A DRAWING FOR YOU

By: _____ Date: _____

By: _____ Date: _____

By: _____ Date: _____

By: _____ Date: _____

By: _____ Date: _____

By: _____ Date: _____

By: _____ Date: _____

By: _____ Date: _____

I WISH YOU WERE HERE TO...

_____

_____

_____

From :_____ Date: _____

YOU WOULD BE GOOD AT...

_____

_____

_____

From : _____ Date: _____

MY WISH FOR YOU...

_____

_____

_____

From : _____ Date: _____

I WISH YOU WERE HERE TO...

_____

_____

_____

From :_____ Date: _____

YOU WOULD BE GOOD AT...

_____

_____

_____

From : _____ Date: _____

MY WISH FOR YOU...

_____

_____

_____

From : _____ Date: _____

I WISH YOU WERE HERE TO...

_____

_____

_____

From :_____ Date: _____

YOU WOULD BE GOOD AT...

_____

_____

_____

From : _____ Date: _____

MY WISH FOR YOU...

_____

_____

_____

From : _____ Date: _____

I WISH YOU WERE HERE TO...

_____

_____

_____

From :_____ Date: _____

YOU WOULD BE GOOD AT...

_____

_____

_____

From : _____ Date: _____

MY WISH FOR YOU...

_____

_____

_____

From : _____ Date: _____

By : _____   Date: _____

By : _____   Date: _____

By : _____   Date: _____

By : _____   Date: _____

By : _____ Date: _____

By : _____ Date: _____

By : _____   Date: _____

By : _____   Date: _____

By: _____ Date: _____

By: _____ Date: _____

Big hugs from
www.harpermartin.com.au

www.ingramcontent.com/pod-product-compliance
Lightning Source LLC
Chambersburg PA
CBHW040316100426
42811CB00012B/1455